THE DAY ELVIS MET NIXON

THE DAY ELVIS MET NIXON

BY EGIL "BUD" KROGH

Former Nixon White House aide

PEJAMA PRESS

To my sons Peter, Jamie and Matthew

PRESIDENT RICHARD NIXON AND
WHITE HOUSE AIDE EGIL KROGH
BRIEF THE WHITE HOUSE PRESS CORPS
ON THE NEW SPECIAL ACTION OFFICE
FOR DRUG ABUSE PREVENTION.

INTRODUCTION Since 1970 I've enjoyed telling the story about the day Elvis Presley met President Nixon. As the White House aide who prepared for and participated in the meeting, I joined in their conversation and saw close up how these two men, who have now achieved the stature of legends in their respective fields, related to each other.

Elvis indicated in his letter to the President that he wanted to help the President on the drug problem. Because drug control policy development was one of my White House responsibilities, I was the aide who got the opportunity to help set up the meeting and take part in it. My drug control responsibilities took me to problem areas in numerous remote parts of the world: the principal poppy-growing province in Turkey; a CIA safe house in Rangoon, Burma; a treatment center for GIs in Can Tho, South Vietnam, to name just a few. I also visited treatment centers in many cities in the United States to try to find out what treatment methodologies were most effective and which could be given more federal support.

While these activities were fascinating and helpful in developing President Nixon's drug control policies, the meeting between Elvis and President Nixon remains in my mind the most novel and interesting. While these two men came from totally different backgrounds, they tried to find ways to cooperate in responding to one of the most severe problems afflicting America's youth. As the meeting took place before the Oval Office taping system had been installed, there are no tapes or transcripts of what was said.

Over the years, many questions have been asked about the meeting. Was Elvis actually "deputized" to fight the drug war? Was he designated an "undercover" agent to assist the Bureau of Narcotics and Dangerous Drugs in its battles? Did he receive an authentic badge from the Bureau that empowered him to take action in case of a drug violation? What did the President and Elvis actually say to each other and how did they get along?

In answering these questions and telling this story about the meeting, I have taken the liberty of quoting the conversations that I had myself or observed firsthand. While I have relied on my notes from the meeting, as well as my hopefully clear memory of the event, I don't claim that all direct quotes represent exactly what was said in the meeting or at other times during the day. But I'm comfortable that the words I've quoted are pretty close.

The purpose of this book is simply to let a broader audience than just visitors to my law office enjoy the inside White House story of why the meeting was set up, how it was organized, and of what actually was said and took place.

A final note. I was and am a fan of Elvis Presley. His songs touched me as they did and still do millions of others. I hope that my fellow fans will enjoy this little story about a day when "The King" was still on his throne and the subjects in his realm could still sway in live concerts to the driving beat and sweetness of his melodies.

Bud Krogh

RICHARD NIXON

577 CHESTNUT RIDGE ROAD
WOODCLIFF LAKE, NEW JERSEY

To Fans of the King:

I am pleased to be able to congratulate Bud Krogh on the publication of *The Day Elvis Met Nixon*.

When we met in the Oval Office in December, 1970, I was greatly impressed by Elvis's sincerity as he described his concerns about the negative influences on young people during that turbulent era of the Vietnam War. This account of how the meeting was planned and what was discussed shatters many of the myths that have been spread by the media.

It also highlights the outstanding staff work done by then (and still) young people in the Nixon White House such as Bud Krogh. Because of their extraordinary efficiency and diligence, Bud and his colleagues were known as miracle workers. It remains to be seen, however, whether the author of *The Day Elvis Met Nixon* will be resourceful enough to be able to arrange for Elvis to appear at a book-signing!

Richard Nixon
4-14-'94

EIGHT DAYS AFTER HE WROTE THIS LETTER TO FANS OF THE KING, RICHARD NIXON PASSED AWAY. HIS LETTER TRULY REFLECTS HIS HUMOR AND GENEROUS SPIRIT. I WILL ALWAYS BE GRATEFUL TO MR. NIXON FOR HIS KINDNESS TO ME.
— BUD KROGH, APRIL 23, 1994

"THE KING IS HERE"

8:45 AM   Dwight Chapin called me about 8:45 in the morning, December 21, 1970.

"Hi, Bud. This is Dwight. Are you sitting down?"

"Yeah, I think so. What's up?"

"You won't believe this, but the King is here. Right here!"

An enthusiastic call from Chapin at 8:45 a.m. wasn't a typical part of my morning, but I rallied and decided to play along.

"King who? No kings on the President's schedule today."

"No, not just any two-bit king," he answered. "*The* King. Elvis, the King of Rock. I'm reading a letter right now he wrote to the President asking for a meeting."

"Come on, Dwight," I said, not really believing what he was telling me. "It's going to be a long day."

Dwight Chapin was one of my best friends in the White House. Known as "Slick" to his campaign buddies for his perfect grooming and movie star good looks, Dwight was a brilliant political strategist, a whirlwind of energy, and one of the men on the staff who knew what the President wanted. More importantly, he knew what Bob Haldeman, the White House Chief

Dear Mr. President.

First, I would like to introduce myself. I am Elvis Presley and admire you and have great respect for your office. I talked to Vice President Agnew in Palm Springs three weeks ago and expressed my concern for our country. The drug culture, the hippie elements, the SDS, Black Panthers, etc. do not consider me as their enemy or as they call it The Establishment. I call it America and I love it. Sir, I can and will be of any service that I can to help The Country out. I have no concern or Motives other than helping the country out. So I wish not to be given a title or an appointed position. I can and will do more good if I were made a Federal Agent at Large and I will help out by doing it my way through my communications with people of all ages. First and foremost, I am an entertainer, but all I need is the Federal credentials. I am on this plane with Senator George Murphy and we have been discussing the problems that our country is faced with.

Sir, I am staying at the Washington Hotel, Room 505-506-507. I have two men who work with me by the name of Jerry Schilling and

of Staff, would approve. We belonged to a small group of White House aides who were close friends and who regularly played radical practical jokes on each other. I had cause for caution.

"No, really, Bud," he continued. "Elvis is here in town. He just gave a handwritten letter to one of the guards at the Northwest Gate. He wants to see the President today."

"Whatever for?" I asked. "Does he want to entertain the troops or something?"

"No, no. His letter talks about wanting to help out on drugs and stuff. I've just red-tagged a copy of his letter to you. Look it over and let me know if you think a meeting makes any sense."

"OK, I'll look it over. What time could we get on the President's schedule?" I asked.

"We've got some time from 11:30 to 12:30 during Open Hour. I suppose we could just have him see Vice President Agnew, but Elvis said in his letter he's already seen him, and we might lose out on a great opportunity. One other thing," Dwight said, "Elvis wants this kept quiet if we can pull it off."

"I'll look his letter over and give you a call. There's not much time to set this up if we decide to do it," I answered and hung up the phone.

I wasn't too sure Dwight was leveling with me. The opportunity for the President to have a shot at reaching young people through a certifiable rock star seemed too good to be true. Since early in 1969, the White House had enlisted the help of celebrities in the Administration's anti-drug campaign. Government officials, from the White House or other agencies, seemed inherently noncredible to the young people we most hoped to reach.

Those of us responsible for the Administration's anti-drug policy felt it was important for people to hear about the hazards of drugs from those not part of the government. Art Linkletter, Roger Staubach, Jack Webb, and Billy Graham had all come to the White House at various times to lend their names and support for the Administration's programs. They were all part of the Establishment, but were the only ones who offered to help us.

Elvis Presley, I thought, might be able to open a pretty good channel to young people. I didn't know how we could keep a meeting secret given the nature of the White House with reporters all over the place, but I thought we could try. Neither Elvis' nor the President's constituency would understand why a meeting took place (which has certainly proven to be true since the meeting became known in 1972).

I remembered that during the 1950s Elvis' hit songs were an important part of my life. His singing and hip-swinging on stage challenged the staid norms of that decade, and I became a pretty avid fan. So the chance to meet the man whose music had been such an exciting part of growing up just couldn't be passed up.

A couple of minutes after hanging up the phone, a messenger arrived with a red-tagged envelope from Chapin. (To ensure immediate delivery within the White House, a staffer would clip a red tag onto a document, and call a White House messenger who would come immediately and hand-carry it to the office or person addressed.)

I opened the envelope and took out Elvis' letter written on American Airlines stationery. The handwriting seemed of grade school quality with a rather uninhibited use of capital letters throughout. As I read the letter I was struck by its apparent sincerity. He expressed concern for the country and said that he had done an in-depth study of drug abuse. He wanted "to help the country out." All he was asking for was a federal credential, to be "made a Federal Agent at Large."

Now the Federal Government didn't have "Federal Agents at Large." It had FBI agents, Bureau of Narcotics and Dangerous Drugs agents, Customs agents, Secret Service agents, but no "Federal Agents at Large." The President had authority to do a lot of things, but he couldn't confer a title that didn't exist. So while the President couldn't give Presley what he wanted, this lack of authority didn't seem to me to be a showstopper.

Elvis also wrote that "The drug culture, The Hippie Elements, the SDS, Black Panthers, etc. do <u>not</u> consider me as their enemy or as they call it The Establishment. <u>I call it America and</u> I love it."

This stirring sentence seemed to me to put Elvis pretty squarely in the Administration's political corner. He was saying that he loved "the Establishment" which was the home town of the Nixon Administration. He suggested that he could work "through my communications with people of all ages." He was "right in the middle of the whole thing, where I can and will do the most good. I am Glad to help just so long as it is kept very Private."

This latter sentence resolved the question of whether to have a public meeting. If Elvis wanted it private, we could do our best to go along with his request. I was already setting up the meeting in my mind.

I called my secretary, Sondra Green, and asked her to put a call through to Jon Burrows at The Washington Hotel. Elvis had written that he was staying there under that name with Jerry Schilling and Sonny West, his bodyguards, in rooms 505-506-507.

When Jerry Schilling came on the line, I said, "Mr. Schilling, my name is Bud Krogh, and I'm on the President's staff. I've just read Mr. Presley's letter, and if he's got some time, I'd like to meet with him in about half an hour. Could you arrange for him to come over to the Old Executive Office Building? It's the big gray building just to the west of the White House."

Schilling sounded very enthusiastic. "Yes, I'm sure he can come! Is it OK if Sonny West and I come with Elvis?"

I told him that would be OK, gave him specific directions about how to get to my office and clear security, and hung up. It was then about 9:30 a.m. I called Dwight.

"Dwight, I've just spoken to Presley's bodyguard. Elvis will be here in about half an hour. His letter seems pretty sincere. I'm going to try and find out what he really wants, and then if it looks good, and Haldeman approves, I'll do a memo for the President. OK?"

"Yeah, that's good, Bud. I've already sent a memo to Haldeman telling him what Presley wants and recommending that we have a meeting with the President during Open Hour. I'll let you know right away if Bob approves. If your meeting with Elvis works out and you think it's OK, we'll do it."

My office, the place where I was soon to meet Elvis, was in Room 171 on the second floor of the Old Executive Office Building. It overlooked the front lawn of the White House and the West Wing where the President's most senior staff members had their offices. The President had a hideaway office in the Old Executive Office Building, two doors away from my office, which he used for study and reflection. If there were to be a meeting, I was sure it would be in the Oval Office, not in his hideaway.

My desk faced into my office, a high-ceilinged, grand old room that was painted light yellow. Dark blue carpeting covered the floor. My furniture consisted of a large table which served as my desk, a long, light blue couch, four soft chairs and a dark wood coffee table. White House staff

---

[Inset document 1 — memorandum, page 2]

2.

I have talked to Bud Korgh about this whole matter, and we both think that it would be wrong to push Presley off on the Vice President since it will take very little of the President's time and it can be extremely beneficial for the President to build some rapport with Presley.

In addition, if the President wants to meet with some bright young people outside of the Government, Presley might be a perfect one to *You must be kidding* start with.

Approve Presley coming in at end of Open Hour _____ *H.*

Disapprove _____

[Inset document 2 — White House memorandum]

THE WHITE HOUSE
WASHINGTON

December 21, 1970

MEMORANDUM FOR: MR. H. R. HALDEMAN

FROM: DWIGHT L. CHAPIN

SUBJECT: Elvis Presley

Attached you will find a letter to the President from Elvis Presley. As you are aware, Presley showed up here this morning and has requested an appointment with the President. He states that he knows the President is very busy, but he would just like to say hello and present the President with a gift.

As you are well aware, Presley was voted one of the ten outstanding young men for next year and this was based upon his work in the field of drugs. The thrust of Presley's letter is that he wants to become a "Federal agent at large" to work against the drug problem by communicating with people of all ages. He says that he is not a member of the establishment and that drug culture types, the hippie elements, the SDS, and the Black Panthers are people with whom he can communicate since he is not part of the establishment.

I suggest that we do the following:

This morning Bud Krogh will have Mr. Presley in and talk to him about drugs and about what Presley can do. Bud will also check to see if there is some kind of an honorary agent at large or credential of some sort that we can provide for Presley. After Bud has met with Presley, it is recommended that we have Bud bring Presley in during the Open Hour to meet briefly with the President. You know that several people have mentioned over the past few months that Presley is very pro the President. He wants to keep everything private and I think we should honor his request.

members could request a certain style of furnishing so long as it was basically consistent with a colonial Williamsburg look, and mine was consistent.

I swung around from my desk to the credenza and started to type out some ideas for a memo to the President. Practically every meeting with the President had to be approved by Bob Haldeman. It was standard procedure in the White House for the responsible staff person to draft a memo to the President explaining the purpose of the meeting, who would participate, and listing some talking points the President might use. Most formal meetings with the President with new guests would follow the script written by the staff person. The staff member would usually meet beforehand with the guest, find out what he or she wanted to say, suggest some talking points, and then write a memo to the President sketching out what the meeting would be about. It was like writing a stage play that would open and close on the same day, and hoping the performance didn't deviate too widely from the script.

And always lurking in the back of your mind was the President's security. You wanted to be sure any guest you sponsored wouldn't do something crazy.

Usually, there was a lot of time to prepare for a meeting with the President. But not that morning. I was in a white heat of creativity trying to figure out how to justify the meeting. My first thought was that Elvis could "work with White House staff." That would ensure that I'd get a chance to see him once in a while. As I put down a few more points, Sondra buzzed me on the intercom and told me that Elvis and his bodyguards were in the lobby. As they had been pre-cleared with security, they would arrive in my office momentarily. The King of Rock was here.

"I LOVE MY COUNTRY..."

10:10 AM   I got up from my chair and walked through to the small adjoining office where Sondra had her desk and where my guests would arrive. I opened the door to the long hallway and saw Elvis and his two muscular bodyguards heading towards me. I waved them towards my office door.

As they came up, I stuck out my hand which had turned cold out of nervousness. "Hi, I'm Bud Krogh. It's real nice to meet you, Mr. Presley."

Elvis shook my hand and said, "It's good to meet you. This here is Sonny West and Jerry Schilling." I shook hands with both of them, and we went into Sondra's office. She was standing in front of her desk with a big smile and was introduced to the three of them.

We went into my office and Elvis sat down on the couch. I sat in the chair next to the couch, and Sonny and Jerry took the two chairs facing the couch across the coffee table.

As soon as I had seen Elvis' clothes, I thought, "Uh-oh. This could get a little dicey." He sure wasn't wearing the standard attire for male guests to the Nixon White House, which was usually church black, dark gray, or blue business suits with white shirts.

But in his own rock star way, he was resplendent. He was wearing tight-fitting dark velvet pants, a white silky shirt with very high collars and open to below his chest, a dark purple velvet cape, a gold medallion, and heavy silver-plated amber-tinted designer sunglasses with "EP" built into the nose bridge. Around his waist was a belt with a huge four-inch by six-inch gold belt buckle with a complex design I couldn't make out without embarrassing myself. Jerry Schilling wore a heavy leather jacket and Sonny West wore a dark suit with an open-necked shirt and a gold chain with a medallion. This was a time in sartorial history when gold chains festooned the necks of many of the more style-conscious men in our society. However, gold chains hadn't quite made their way onto the necks of male staff members in the White House, at least during working hours.

I opened our conversation. "Mr. Presley, as I mentioned on the phone, I've read your letter. If possible, we'd like to see if we can schedule a meeting with the President around noon today. We could sure use your help with the President's drug program. It's very hard for us to reach young people around the country."

Elvis answered somewhat formally, almost as if it had been rehearsed: "I love my country, and I care a lot about my family and friends. I'd like to do what I can to help out. I didn't try to get out of the Army because that was my duty. And it was the right thing to do. I'd like to pay back the country for a lot that's been given to me." It sounded to me like Elvis was auditioning for a part, and in a way he was. He obviously knew that he and I had to have a good meeting for the meeting with the President to take place.

"Well," I said, "We've tried here in the government to reach out to young people and explain the tremendous dangers with drugs, especially heroin. We've just heard that as of last week, over a thousand people in New York City alone have died this year from narcotics, and a couple of hundred of these were teenagers." These statistics were close to my mind as I intended to use them as "talking points" in my memo to the President—which was still in draft form in my typewriter.

Elvis nodded and said, "I think I can help with teenagers. Not in any direct way. Just through my music and other ways I can communicate. I'm pretty accepted by everyone."

"That would be very helpful if you can do it," I replied. "We've had some good help from a couple of disk jockeys, Murray the K and Cousin Brucey. They came to the White House to lend us a hand at the suggestion of Art Buchwald. Jeff Donfeld on the staff here spent a day with them and a few others to describe the huge scope of the drug problem as we see it."

Elvis continued, "I've also tried to help the guys in law enforcement around the country. They're on the front lines. I drop in on police departments once in a while. I've got a lot of badges in my collection from police and sheriffs around the country."

"Well, the police sure have their hands full," I replied. "We're going to add a thousand new police to the force here in D.C. The crime problem here in the District is just awful, and a lot of it is due to drugs."

Throughout our conversation, Elvis kept scratching at his neck. "I've got this rash, see, that's been bothering me for a while. But it's no problem." I noticed that his hair was almost brittle from hair spray. He looked pretty uncomfortable and moved around on the couch while he talked.

"If I can, I'd like to tell the President that I want to help him and the country out. That's my only purpose. And if I can get some kind of credential, that would be great," he said.

There wasn't much time to discuss anything more if we were going to make the meeting happen. "Well," I said, "We'll have to see how it goes and how the folks around here feel about it." After saying this, I got up. Elvis, Sonny and Jerry followed me out to the hallway. "Why don't you go back to your hotel now. We should get word pretty quick about the meeting. If it's a 'Go' you'll need to get back here pretty fast. Either way, I'll let you know as soon as I get the word." We all shook hands and they left with smiles for Sondra. It was about 10:15 a.m.

"HALDEMAN APPROVED THE MEETING, BOB"

10:15 AM   As soon as they left, I rushed back to my typewriter and continued banging out points in my memo to the President. I called Jeff Donfeld, the White House staff member most knowledgeable about all aspects of the Administration's drug program, and asked him for some further suggestions for the President's memo. We thought that it might be helpful if Elvis were to participate in a TV special about the drug themes in rock music, or encourage other artists to develop a rock musical with a "Get High on Life" theme. I also included in the memo a somewhat fatuous suggestion that Elvis record an album with the "Get High on Life" theme at the federal narcotic rehabilitation and research facility at Lexington, Kentucky.

Perhaps our respective muses were having an off day, but in the heat of the moment, when you've got to get talking points down on paper fast, there isn't much time to research ideas very thoroughly. I finished the memo to the President with the suggestion that Elvis serve as a consultant to the Advertising Council on how to communicate anti-drug messages to youth. Sondra then typed up my draft in a few minutes, and it was red-tagged over to Dwight. He called me back right away after reading it.

"Haldeman approved the meeting, Bud. How did your session with the King go?"

"It went great," I said. "I think he's really sincere and wants to help out. I heard the whole story about his not wanting to duck out of serving in the Army. Pretty darned impressive. But you should see what he's wearing. Dark cape. White shirt open. Gold chain. All he needs is his guitar and he could perform right in the Oval Office."

"Oh, well, that'll just add some color to the meeting," Dwight laughed. "Have him here a little before noon. We should be able to get him in around 12:30. OK?"

"Yeah, that's great," I replied. "This is turning out to be a very weird day. Talk to you later."

I hung up the phone and reread the memo I'd just finished for the President. I had pointed out that Jimi Hendrix and Janis Joplin, two explosively talented and popular rock stars, had died within two weeks of each other. While it wasn't certain, their deaths were reportedly from drug-related causes. I wasn't sure the President would have known about them, but I wanted him to understand how the drug problem hit people personally. So much of the drug problem as viewed from government was just a litany of grim statistics, as reflected in the third of my "talking points" about 1,022 narcotics deaths in New York City alone.

THE WHITE HOUSE
WASHINGTON
December 21, 1970

MEMORANDUM FOR: THE PRESIDENT

SUBJECT: Meeting with Elvis Presley
December 21, 1970
12:30 p.m.

I. PURPOSE

To thank Elvis Presley for his offer to help in trying to stop the drug epidemic in the country, and to ask him to work with us in bringing a more positive attitude to young people throughout the country.

In his letter to you, Elvis Presley offered to help as much as possible with the growing drug problem. He requested the meeting with you this morning when he presented himself to the guard at the Northwest Gate bearing a letter.

II. PARTICIPANTS

Elvis Presley

Bud Krogh (staff)

III. TALKING POINTS

A. We have asked the entertainment industry - both television and radio - to assist us in our drug fight.

B. You are aware that the average American family has 4 radio sets; 98% of the young people between 12 and 17 listen to radio. Between the time a child is born and he leaves high school, it is estimated he watches between 15,000 and 20,000 hours of television. That is more time than he spends in the classroom.

-2-

C. The problem is critical: As of December 14, 1970, 1,022 people died this year in New York alone from just narcotic related deaths. 208 of these were teenagers.

D. Two of youth's folk heroes, Jimi Hendrix and Janis Joplin, recently died within a period of two weeks reportedly from drug-related causes. Their deaths are a sharp reminder of how the rock music culture has been linked to the drug sub-culture. If our youth are going to emulate the rock music stars, from now on let those stars affirm their conviction that true and lasting talent is the result of self motivation and discipline and not artificial chemical euphoria.

E. Suggestions for Presley activities:

1. Work with White House Staff

2. Cooperate with and encourage the creation of an hour Television Special in which Presley narrates as stars such as himself sing popular songs and interpret them for parents in order to show drug and other anti-establishment themes in rock music.

3. Encourage fellow artists to develop a new rock musical theme, "Get High on Life."

4. Record an album with the theme "Get High on Life" at the federal narcotic rehabilitation and research facility at Lexington, Kentucky.

5. Be a consultant to the Advertising Council on how to communicate anti-drug messages to youth.

I waited a few more minutes to allow time for Elvis, Jerry and Sonny to get back to their hotel. I then called "Jon Burrows" once again.

"Mr. Schilling," I said when he answered the phone. "This is Bud Krogh again. The President will be happy to meet with Mr. Presley around 12:30 today. Come on back over to the White House around 11:45. Use the Northwest Gate on Pennsylvania Avenue. That's the same gate where Mr. Presley gave his letter to the guard this morning. I'll clear the three of you in again."

"That's great. Thanks very much. We'll see you soon." He hung up. It was about 10:30 a.m.

"BUD, WE'VE GOT A LITTLE PROBLEM..."

10:30 AM My final preparations for the meeting with the President consisted of going over the planned scenario once again with Jeff Donfeld and talking over the earlier meeting with Elvis with my secretary, Sondra Green. We all agreed that the meeting with the President was the right thing to do even though we knew I would be winging it.

Around 11:45, I was interrupted by a tense call from Bill Duncan, the head of the President's Secret Service protective detail.

"Good morning, Bud," he said with an edge in his voice. "We've got a little problem here. Elvis Presley just arrived here in the West Wing lobby with his bodyguards. He wants to give a gun to the President as a gift."

"He wants to give *what*?" I asked. This was alarming news. Elvis hadn't said anything about giving the President a gun.

"Yeah, we intercepted the gun at the Northwest Gate when they came in. It's a pretty fancy automatic. Nice display case with seven silver bullets inserted at the bottom. Bud, you know we can't let him take a gun into the Oval Office with bullets that may be live."

"Bill, I certainly understand that," I said. "Let me think for a second about what we can do."

Elvis didn't seem to have any dangerous tendencies, and not telling me about the gun was probably just an oversight. I tried to figure out what we could do without endangering the President and offending Elvis. The Secret Service was understandably highly sensitive to any kind of potential threat to the President. The first briefing from the Secret Service right after I joined the President's transition staff in November of 1968 flashed through my mind. The Service was passionately dedicated to avoiding any kind of risk that might lead to a repetition of the "Tragedy." The "Tragedy" was the term used by the Secret Service when discussing the assassination of President Kennedy. It was clear that the gun couldn't be taken into the Oval Office.

"Bill," I said, "I'm on my way over to the lobby right away. Why don't you tell Elvis that security regulations make it impossible to take the gun in, but that you will accept it on behalf of the President. We'll let the President know about it. Will this be OK?"

"Yes, I think that will be fine, Bud. I'll see you in a minute."

I reread the postscript in Elvis' letter to the President. It hadn't really registered with me the first time through. Elvis had written:

I have a personal gift for you also which I would like to present to you and you can accept it or I will keep it for you until you can take it.

At least Elvis recognized that the President might not be able to accept the gun personally, so this would probably mitigate any hurt feelings he might have. As I walked over to the West Wing, I tried to figure out why Elvis would want to present a gun anyway. Maybe it was to show some kind of solidarity with the President's hard line on law enforcement or pro-military views.

I walked into the West Wing lobby and saw Elvis, Sonny and Jerry standing near the entrance.

"Good morning, again, Mr. Presley. Are you ready?"

"Yeah, I sure am," he answered with a big smile.

"I hope you understand why your gift can't be taken into the Oval Office. No guns in the Oval Office is standard policy around here."

"Sure, I understand, Bud. I just thought the President would like to have a gun like that. It's a real collector's gun." Bill Duncan by this time had already taken custody of the gun in its display case on behalf of the President.

"I'm sure he'll appreciate it," I said. "A beautiful gift like that usually ends up being prominently displayed in the Presidential library after the President leaves office. Everyone who visits the library will get a chance to see it and appreciate it."

It turned out that's exactly what happened to the gun Elvis gave President Nixon. It's currently on display as Exhibit 119 in the Nixon Library in Yorba Linda, California. The gun is a chrome-plated Colt .45 with a wood handle with the following display inscription:

WW II Commemorative European/African Middle Eastern Theatre, December 11, 1941 - May 7, 1943.

On the gun itself, several battle areas are inscribed:

North Atlantic, Tunisia, Sicily, Plusto, Anzio, Normandy, Bastogne, Remagen, Berlin.

With the mini-crisis over the gun resolved, I repeated to Elvis how important a contribution he could make to the country's anti-drug fight. He seemed very eager to help and almost hyper-excited about the meeting.

He showed me the two autographed pictures he wanted to give the President. One of him and his wife, Priscilla; the other of their baby, Lisa Marie, wearing a full baby bonnet. He was also clutching a handful of police badges from various police departments and sheriff's offices around the country that he wanted the President to see. A few minutes later, Nell Yates, the receptionist in the West Wing lobby, told me to bring Elvis to the Oval Office. It was 12:30 p.m.

"SHOW & TELL...AND ASK"

12:30 PM   Elvis and I walked through the Roosevelt Room and across the hall to the northwest door to the Oval Office. A Secret Service agent, who was stationed there when the President was in his office, greeted us. He opened the door and I ushered Elvis in.

Entering the Oval Office for the first time to meet the President can be a rather intimidating experience for almost anyone. My first visit to brief the President sure had intimidated me. That meeting had taken place in January of 1969, a couple of days after the Inauguration. I was asked to brief the President on the government's proposed policy for dealing with anti-war demonstrations and protests. This issue was under the jurisdiction of the Counsel to the President, John Ehrlichman, and he had assigned specific responsibility to me.

I remember entering the Oval Office and seeing the President reclining in his chair behind his desk with his feet crossed on the desktop. Because I was just a staff person joining an informal meeting already in progress with Ehrlichman, there wasn't any reason for the President to get up. I took a chair directly in front of the desk, and found myself staring at the soles of the President's shoes. His face was totally blocked out.

During that first visit of mine, I remember Ehrlichman saying, "Mr. President, Bud Krogh here has been responsible for developing our policy on protests here in D.C. Let him give you a rundown on what we're doing."

The President then simply widened the split between his crossed shoes, and I found myself staring into his face framed by the "V" of his soles. For a split second, all my cognitive and communicative functions ceased. The President of the United States was looking at *me* for information. Fortunately, I had taken the precaution of writing down on a yellow pad the leading points I wanted to make. After glancing down at them, I was able to get a few words out which enabled me to get rolling on the briefing. The initial panic, however, had been real.

While Elvis' reaction on entering the Oval Office wasn't exactly panic, it nevertheless wasn't what I had expected. He was one of the most famous individuals in the world, someone who had entertained millions of people. I expected him to be immediately at ease on entering the Oval Office. Such was not the case.

He walked in a step in front of me and stopped. He looked up at the ceiling, which had a large eagle emblazoned in the plaster. He looked down at the blue carpeting on the floor which had another eagle centered in the Presidential seal. Eagles adorned the tops of the armed services flags to the right of the President's desk. The Presidential seal that had been embroidered by Julie Eisenhower during the 1968 campaign and given to him in the early hours right after he had "gone over the top" to win the election was hanging on the wall just to the right of the door Elvis entered. I noticed Elvis observe everything and then hesitantly walk forward to greet the President. He seemed to be awed if not over-whelmed by it all.

President Nixon got up from his chair as we entered the room and walked around his desk to meet Elvis. He was wearing a gray suit with the American flag in his lapel. Ollie Atkins, the White House photographer, began taking pictures as soon as they reached each other. Because the meeting was to be brief, known in White House parlance as a "drop-by," there was no plan to sit down in the couches which faced each other in front of the fireplace or in the chairs on either side of the President's desk.

As they started to shake hands, I said, "Mr. President, this is Mr. Elvis Presley." Elvis was still wearing his sunglasses and holding the badges and pictures in his left hand.

They continued shaking hands for a few seconds while Ollie Atkins snapped their picture. The President then started the conversation: "It's very good to meet you, Mr. Presley. I appreciate your offer to help us on the drug problem." While to the world, Elvis Presley was thought of simply as Elvis, in the very formal White House of 1970, he was addressed as Mr. Presley. Elvis didn't respond to

the President's greeting, but just kept smiling. So I jumped in. "Mr. President, Mr. Presley has told me that he can reach a lot of young people through his music to help them stay off or get off drugs." I tried to get the conversation underway by mentioning something Elvis earlier had told me he wanted to say.

After a few awkward seconds, Elvis said: "Mr. President, thank you for seeing me. I'd like to show you some pictures of my family and some of my badges." After saying this, he stepped over to the President's desk and spread out his badges and pictures. The President stood next to him.

Elvis selected first the picture of Priscilla and himself and handed it to the President. The President picked it up and smiled. Elvis then said, "And here's a picture of my daughter, Lisa Marie," as he handed her picture to the President. Elvis seemed to be getting over his initial shyness.

"She's a beautiful little girl," the President said. Elvis smiled.

Elvis then picked up various police badges and started showing them to the President. "I have a collection of badges from police departments around the country," he said. "I really support what our police have to do." The President responded: "They certainly deserve all the support we can give them. They've got tough jobs."

The President then said: "Mr. Presley, let's let Ollie take some pictures over here." The President then directed Elvis to a position in front of the military service flags, and Ollie Atkins took a number of pictures of them there. This position in the Oval Office was a popular place for taking pictures of the President and his guests.

They stepped back to the desk where Elvis pulled up his sleeve to show him his cuff links.

The President bent over Elvis' right arm to get a good look at the cuff link. I was standing several feet away observing this and taking down notes of what they said.

Elvis continued by saying, "I've been performing a lot in Las Vegas. Quite a place." The President responded with a smile. "I know very well how difficult it is to play Las Vegas," he said. I didn't know what campaign visit the President was alluding to or what he had heard from his friends in the entertainment industry that prompted this comment.

The President continued: "As Bud mentioned, Mr. Presley, I think you can reach young people in a way no one in the government can. It's important that you keep your credibility." It seemed that the President was becoming concerned that the visit remain confidential so that Elvis' credibility, and perhaps his own, would not be impaired.

Elvis answered: "I do my thing just by singing, Mr. President. I don't make any speeches on stage. I just try to reach them in my own way." The President nodded his agreement to this.

The conversation then took an odd turn. Elvis said: "The Beatles, I think, are kind of anti-American. They came over here. Made a lot of money. And then went back to England. And they said some anti-American stuff when they got back."

I didn't have a clue what Elvis was referring to. He hadn't brought up the Beatles at all in our earlier meeting. From the look of surprise on the President's face when Elvis said this, I was convinced the President didn't know what he was talking about either. Maybe there was an element of jealousy in Presley's comment as by the time of the meeting with the President, the Beatles were the hottest rock group in the world and had eclipsed Elvis in popularity for some younger fans.

The President then said: "You know, those who use the drugs are the protesters. You know, the ones who get caught up in dissent and violence. They're the same group of young people."

"Mr. President," Elvis said, "I'm on your side. I want to be helpful. And I want to help get people to respect the flag because that's getting lost."

The flag was also a new topic. I wasn't sure what precipitated this comment. Maybe it was the American flag in the President's lapel, or the armed services flags, or the stories of flag burning which Elvis probably had heard. Whatever the cause, it was clear Elvis was trying to find things to say that the President would approve of.

"I'm just a poor boy from Tennessee. I've gotten a lot from my country. And I'd like to do something to repay for what I've gotten."

"That will be very helpful," the President replied. "We need a lot of help on this drug problem."

Elvis continued: "I've been studying Communist brainwashing for over ten years now, and the drug culture, too."

This last comment took us into uncharted waters. I could see the President was having a hard time, as was I, in following the linkage between Communist brainwashing and the drug culture. I thought it would be prudent to bring the conversation back to a safer harbor.

"Mr. President," I said, "Mr. Presley told me that he's accepted by many of those we'd like to reach with our anti-drug message."

The President nodded again, and Elvis said: "I can go right into a group of hippies and young people and be accepted. This can be real helpful."

The President paused before replying: "Well, that's fine. But just be sure you don't lose your credibility."

Elvis then asked a question that caught me by surprise.

"Mr. President, can you get me a badge from the Narcotics Bureau? I've been trying to get a badge from them for my collection." He pointed again to some of the police badges he had put on the President's desk. In the earlier meeting in my office, Elvis had told me about his support for police and law enforcement departments around the country. He said he liked to drop in on police departments by surprise, and give a gift of cash or some other expensive item. The police would then often give him a badge in return. While he had mentioned he wanted "some kind of credential," he hadn't specified a badge from the Bureau of Narcotics and Dangerous Drugs.

The President looked a little uncertain at this request. He turned to me and asked, "Bud, can we get him a badge?"

I couldn't read what the President really wanted me to say.

"Well, sir," I answered, "If you want to give him a badge, I think we can get him one."

The President nodded. "I'd like to do that. See that he gets one."

"Yes, sir," I responded.

Elvis was smiling triumphantly. "Thank you very much, sir. This means a lot to me." He seemed to be energized if not overcome by this. "Mr. President, I really do support what you're doing, and I want to help."

Elvis then moved up close to the President and, in a spontaneous gesture, put his left arm around him and hugged him. President hugging was not, at least in my limited experience, a common occurrence in the Oval Office. It caught the President—and me—off guard. The President recovered from his surprise and patted Elvis on the shoulder. "Well, I appreciate your willingness to help us out, Mr. Presley."

Elvis then went back to the desk. "I'd like you to have these pictures. And I also brought a gift for you, a real fine collector's World War II Colt .45. The Secret Service guy received it for you."

"Thank you very much," the President said. "That's very kind of you."

Elvis then scooped up his badges and turned to go. He looked like a kid who had just received all of the Christmas presents he'd asked for. He turned back to the President.

"Mr. President, would you have a little time just to say hello to my two friends, Sonny West and Jerry Schilling? It would mean a lot to them and to me."

The President looked at me. "Bud, do we have time for that?" The President knew that during Open Hour visitors get stacked up pretty tightly.

"Yes, sir," I said, flying blindly. "I think we have a few more minutes." I thought that Sonny and Jerry would enjoy meeting the President and it seemed a shame to spoil the ebullient mood. "I'll go get them."

I walked over to the door and asked the agent to bring Sonny and Jerry to the Oval Office. When they walked in, they looked both delighted and a little dazed. As we came over to the desk, the President shook hands with them both. I had asked that Ollie Atkins return to the office. He took pictures of Elvis, Sonny and Jerry with the President.

The President said, as he was shaking hands, "You've got a couple of big ones here, Elvis."

"They're good friends, Mr. President. And they are interested in helping you out, too."

"I appreciate what you're all doing," the President said. "As I said before, just be sure you keep your credibility." He then walked around to the front of his desk and opened the bottom left hand drawer. In this drawer the President kept gifts he could give to his visitors.

"Let's see here," said the President. "Here are some tie clasps." The tie clasps had the

Presidential seal on them, and while they were probably great gifts for most men, I wasn't sure Elvis, Sonny or Jerry even owned any ties. Elvis, obviously curious about what else was in the drawer, walked over behind the desk. He and the President started rummaging through the drawer together.

"Remember, Mr. President, they've got wives," Elvis said, picking up some pins with the Presidential seal on them. Golf balls, cuff links, and pins were laid on the desk. I'm not sure which gifts were finally given, but after the raid on the drawer, Elvis, Sonny and Jerry had their hands full. They all seemed delighted with what they had received.

The President then escorted them to the door. "Thank you very much, fellas," he said.

Elvis, Sonny, and Jerry all thanked the President, shook hands, and I then guided them into the hall by the Secret Service agent's desk. The agent got up and closed the door. It was 1:05 p.m.

"POWER LUNCH"

Elvis, Sonny and Jerry couldn't stop smiling as we walked across the hall.

"That was great, Elvis," Sonny said. "I didn't think we'd get a chance to see him." It was clear that for both Sonny and Jerry, getting in to see the President was much more than either of them had expected. And not only had they received a handful of gifts for themselves and their wives, Elvis had gotten the prize he most desired—a promise from the President to get a badge from the Bureau of Narcotics and Dangerous Drugs.

"Would you like some lunch here in the White House mess?" I asked, looking for a way to extend Elvis' visit a little longer.

"Yeah, we sure would," Elvis replied.

I led them back through the Roosevelt Room, one of the formal rooms in the West Wing of the White House, directly across from the Oval Office. Hanging on the north wall of the Roosevelt Room was a picture of Teddy Roosevelt in his Rough Rider uniform storming San Juan Hill. The Domestic Council staff met in the Roosevelt Room every weekday morning at 7:30 a.m., and as a member of that staff I was well familiar with the room. I pointed out the pictures and explained how the room was used by the President and the staff for informal meetings and an occasional press briefing or photo opportunity.

While Elvis, Sonny and Jerry looked around the room, I stopped at a table with a phone and put a call through to John Finlator, the Deputy Director of the Bureau of Narcotics and Dangerous Drugs. When he came on the line I said, "John, Elvis just met with the President about helping out with our drug program."

"Yes, I heard he had a meeting with the President set up. He came here after meeting with you this morning," he replied.

"Could you come over to my office around 2:00?" I asked. "We're going to have some lunch first. And, John, please bring one of your agent badges. The President wants to give him one."

"OK, OK, Bud. I'll see you at 2:00."

After the call we proceeded down the stairs to the basement level of the West Wing. Staff members, secretaries, and security types seemed stunned when we passed them in the hallway.

Just inside the basement entrance to the West Wing, I pointed out the door that led to the Situation Room, a small conference room at the back of several offices which seemed like 24-hour-a-day homes for the busiest members of Henry Kissinger's National Security Council staff. I explained to Elvis that in that room many national security crises had been resolved by senior officials of the military, the diplomatic service, and the intelligence services. All three seemed impressed at the high security protecting the entrance to the Situation Room.

We passed the White House police officer who sits at a desk inside the basement entrance next to the door leading to the Situation Room, and headed down the hallway to the mess.

At that time, the White House mess was an official Navy mess which served basic good food three meals a day. Many staff members ate all three meals there when workloads demanded it, which happened frequently. Filipino stewards were assigned as waiters, and many of them had served there for many years.

The mess had wood panelling, dark wood tables and chairs, and green carpet. Two large round tables where individual staff members could eat were in the corners. Tables for two were set against the walls, and tables for four were in the middle of the room.

When we walked into the mess to be seated, I noticed the stares, many of them open-mouthed, from other staff members who were already eating. Even though White House staff members were accustomed to seeing heads of state, athletic champions, and movie stars, Elvis was still the King to many of them and in a class of royalty by himself. They all gaped.

A steward showed us to a table for four in the middle of the room. Elvis stood by one of the chairs. Jerry Schilling stepped behind him, took off Elvis' cape, and then held his chair for him. Elvis sat down. He looked around the room, responding with smiles to the stares.

It would be difficult to describe all of the emotions running through my mind at that moment. Hosting the King of Rock in the White House mess in front of many of my friends was clearly the highlight of that day, or year. It was thrilling and funny, serious and a little embarrassing.

Our conversation went back to our meeting with the President and I picked up the main theme of the meeting.

"You know, Mr. Presley, I think you have a real opportunity to help the country. As the President said, you can reach those young people we can't reach."

"That's what I want to do," Elvis replied. "Help the country out."

I then explained what the Administration was trying to do with its program on drugs.

"One of the areas that has been seriously neglected," I said, "is the educational side, and those programs dealing with rehabilitation and treatment. We've always had a heavy emphasis on law enforcement. We're now developing ways to get more federal money into the 'demand' side and to get more of a balance between law enforcement and treatment."

Elvis listened closely to this. "Well, as I told the President, I can help the most by just talking with people."

I agreed that that was where he could do the most good.

What we actually ate for lunch didn't really register with me even while eating it. When we finished, we walked along the corridor back to the police desk by the West Wing entrance. Some secretaries were lined up to get his autograph which Elvis gave with a smile for each.

We walked back across West Executive Drive, into the Old Executive Office Building, and up the stairs to my office. Elvis seemed almost manic about how well the meeting with the President had gone. He darted in and out of several offices on the second floor, and in one of them gave the startled secretary a hug where she sat at her desk.

When we arrived back at my office, Jeff Donfeld joined us and we debriefed him on our meeting with the President.

"Jeff," I said, "the President directed that Elvis get a badge from BNDD. I called Finlator and asked him to bring over a badge. He should be here around 2:00."

After a few more minutes, Sondra told me that John Finlator had arrived. Jeff and I greeted him in my outer office.

"You know how these things go, John," I said. "Elvis' request caught me a little off guard. But the President wanted to give him a badge."

"OK, Bud," Finlator said and smiled, "being reversed by the President isn't too bad."

The three of us went back into my office and Finlator handed a badge to Elvis and promised to send him a consultant's commission later. Elvis thanked him profusely.

After Finlator left I said, "Mr. Presley, thank you very much for all your help. It's been a real pleasure meeting you."

Elvis responded, "Thank you, Bud, for setting this up. I really appreciate all of it." Sonny and Jerry also thanked me for their meeting with the President.

We shook hands and said goodbye in front of my office, and then Elvis, Jerry and Sonny headed down the second floor corridor, leaving the White House for good.

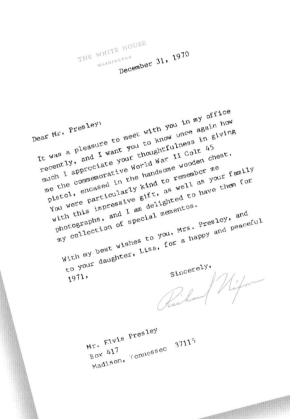

THE WHITE HOUSE
WASHINGTON
December 31, 1970

Dear Mr. Presley:

It was a pleasure to meet with you in my office recently, and I want you to know once again how much I appreciate your thoughtfulness in giving me the commemorative World War II Colt 45 pistol, encased in the handsome wooden chest. You were particularly kind to remember me with this impressive gift, as well as your family photographs, and I am delighted to have them for my collection of special mementos.

With my best wishes to you, Mrs. Presley, and to your daughter, Lisa, for a happy and peaceful 1971,

Sincerely,

Richard Nixon

Mr. Elvis Presley
Box 417
Madison, Tennessee 37115

"TOP SECRET"

EPILOGUE   In retrospect, it seems incredible that Elvis Presley could come to the White House twice that day, meet with the President, walk the halls of both the West Wing and the Old Executive Office Building, eat lunch in the White House mess, talk to numerous staff members and secretaries and not have one word appear in the press about it for over a year. Not until Jack Anderson described the meeting in *The Washington Post* on January 27, 1972, was there any mention in the press about Elvis' day at the White House. The meeting enjoyed more secrecy than most of the "Top Secret" information floating around the White House those days.

I had no occasion to visit with Elvis Presley again. Others have written about what he did with his special badge from the Bureau of Narcotics and Dangerous Drugs. I was disappointed that during my remaining three years on the White House staff, opportunities didn't arise for Elvis to "work with White House staff" as I had hoped for and suggested. I enjoyed the brief time we had together that day. I liked him a lot.

The Washington Merry-Go-Round

THE WASHINGTON POST *Thursday, Jan. 27, 1972* D 23

Presley Gets Narcotics Bureau Badge

By Jack Anderson

By presidential dictum, Elvis Presley, the swivel-hipped singer, has been issued a federal narcotics badge.

The emotional Presley was so overwhelmed at getting his own genuine, gold-plated badge that tears sprang from his eyes, and he grabbed President Nixon in a Hollywood bear hug.

The rock 'n' roll star is a police buff who collects law enforcement badges and donates thousands of dollars to police charities. Hearing of this, Deputy Narcotics Director John Finlator a few months ago sought to enlist Presley in the anti-drug fight.

Finlator invited the singer to the Narcotics Bureau for a quiet visit and arranged for the guards to admit him under the pseudonym "John Burroughs."

Presley played the part of the anonymous John Burroughs like he does all his movie roles. He pulled up in front of the Narcotics Bureau in a gaudy Cadillac. Resplendent in purple suit and cloak, with a gold belt buckle and amber sunglasses, he sashayed through the door.

En route to Finlator's office, the elegant Elvis, alias John Burroughs, had half the secretaries in the building oohing and aahing.

Presley readily agreed to cooperate with the anti-drug campaign and offered on the spot to donate $5,000 to the Narcotics Bureau. Finlator gently declined the money, explaining that the Bureau isn't permitted to accept donations.

Then Presley showed Finlator some police badges and asked whether he could have one from the Narcotics Bureau. Finlator suggested diplomatically that he try the FBI. But Elvis insisted he wanted a narcotics badge.

"I can't," said Finlator apologetically. "I absolutely can't let you have one."

Presley's face fell, then brightened again. He said he had an appointment at the White House. "Would you mind," he asked, "if I asked President Nixon for a narcotics badge?"

"That's the only way you'll ever get it, Elvis," replied Finlator good humoredly.

At the White House, Presley was ushered in to see the President. They chatted briefly, then Presley raised the question of the badge.

"See that he gets it," the President directed his top enforcement adviser, Egil (Bud) Krogh. Unable to suppress his excitement, Elvis hugged the startled Nixon.

Krogh immediately called Finlator and asked him to bring a badge to the White House.

"You know how it is, John," Krogh greeted Finlator later at the White House. "I hear you turned him down."

"I sure as hell did," said Finlator, smiling. "Okay, I've been reversed."

When Finlator finally handed Presley the badge and promised to issue him "consultant" credentials, the singer was overcome with emotion, and his eyes became misty.

It was another happy ending for the swivel 'n' sway idol.

Footnote: Finlator recently retired from the Narcotics Bureau to write a book about his experiences.

The Labor Department has refused to allow the son of murdered United Mine Workers insurgent Jock Y... to speak to a group of government employees ... hear him.

The son, Jo... blonski, is a V... ney who sp... law. He had ... appear by ... manageme... viously, th... to hea... wanted.

The

expected to discuss the ... Department's refusal ... vene when his fathe... for help in ... against UMW ... Boyle in 19...

When ... tary L... hea... he ... tha...

T... cus... is e... the a... ment's ... be-bo... Boy... cor... for... Y... ti...

49

ACKNOWLEDGEMENT   My deepest thanks go to the late Ollie Atkins, the gifted White House photographer during the Nixon years, who took the remarkable pictures of Elvis in the Oval Office. Ollie was loved by everyone on the staff for his quiet competence, kindness and friendliness.

My thanks, too, go to Dwight Chapin who suggested and pushed for the Elvis meeting with President Nixon and to the late Bob Haldeman who wrote, when presented with Dwight's proposal suggesting the meeting, "You must be kidding!" but approved it anyway.

In the design of this book, my thanks go to Widmeyer Design, and particularly Ken Widmeyer and Dale Hart, whose extraordinary talents and creative fire illuminated the path for us during the long hours of putting this book together. In carrying out the responsibilities of publishing this book under the aegis of Pejama Press, my thanks go to my older son, Peter B. Krogh, whose enthusiasm, intelligence, and resourcefulness in solving each problem as it came up were indispensable in getting this story told. I'd also like to thank Valerie Ryan, Laura C. Dail and Gary Lothian for their wise counsel in developing our approach for publishing the book.

For more information about the time leading up to Elvis' White House visit and afterwards, the books by Priscilla Presley entitled *Elvis and Me* and by Jerry Hopkins entitled *Elvis, The Final Years* can help. John Finlator's book, *The Drugged Nation*, describes in great detail on pages 102 to 105, his meeting with Elvis where the King agreed to help with the drug problem. Following the meeting with Finlator and the President, Elvis sent $2,000 to the National Coordinating Council on Drug Education.

In addition to displaying the gun Elvis gave to President Nixon, the Nixon Library in Yorba Linda, California, offers many memorabilia and souvenirs about the meeting between Elvis and President Nixon. Posters, post-cards, t-shirts, watches, books, and other fun souvenirs are all available by calling (714) 993-5070.

Without the opportunity to serve on the White House staff, this book wouldn't have been possible. So my final thanks go to John D. Ehrlichman who hired me out of his Seattle law firm in 1968 to work on the White House staff which I did in various capacities until 1973. And to the late President Richard Nixon who had confidence in me and gave me many fascinating assignments during the time I was on his staff. In Elvis' terms, I wish I could have done a better job of serving them and "helping the country out."